BLUFF YOUR WAY IN COMPUTERS

ROBERT AINSLEY & ALEXANDER C. RAE

D1168001

ℛℛ

RAVETTE PUBLISHING

Published by Ravette Publishing Limited
P.O. Box 296
Horsham
West Sussex RH13 8FH
Telephone: (01403) 711443
Fax: (01403) 711554

First printed 1988
Reprinted 1990
Updated 1991, 1992, reprinted 1993
Revised 1994, reprinted 1995
Updated 1996

Series Editor – Anne Tauté

Cover design – Jim Wire
Printing & binding – Cox & Wyman Ltd.
Production – Oval Projects Ltd.

The Bluffer's Guides® is a
Registered Trademark.

The Bluffer's Guides® series is based
on an original idea by Peter Wolfe.

An **Oval Project**
for Ravette Publishing.

CONTENTS

COMPUTER BLUFF

The more complex and sophisticated computers become, the easier it gets to bluff people into believing that you are a computer expert. Simply cut all words from your conversation except 'the', 'and', 'multimedia' and 'information superhighway', and then fill up the spaces with letters, numbers and meaningless jargon.

The truth is, no-one really knows what they are talking about. Computer users do not have a clue about how the programs they use are written. Computer programmers do not have any idea how the chips running their programs work. And the designers of the chips do not understand why they work. Finding someone who understands everything is like the old Schleswig-Holstein question: only three people knew the answer, and of them one was dead, one had gone mad, and the other had forgotten.

So everyone you meet, however confident they seem at the party, is bluffing to a greater or lesser extent. Except Microsoft chairman Bill Gates, of course, who really does understand everything. But as he is a multi-billionaire you are unlikely to meet him at a party, especially if you are cheap enough to be have down-loaded this off the Internet instead of paying for it like everyone else.

The purpose of this book, then, is to let you bluff to the greatest extent possible, with the minimum amount of knowledge needed to impress and influence people – that is, nothing.

First, just follow our **Golden Rules** to the Complete Computer Buff Bluff.

Golden Rules to Computer Bluffing

1. The **"Today I'm an expert on multimedia"** ploy.

Always be an 'expert' in a different type of area to the one the other person at the party is talking about. If they mention the internet, switch the subject to multimedia. If they want to discuss multimedia, talk about electronic mail instead.

Similarly, if they are talking about computers in a business context, say this is not what is important any more: it is computers in the home. And vice versa. Their subject was important two years ago, but has been overtaken by developments in technology. Your own subject is the most exciting, the potential is vast, and it is where things are all heading.

If you are surrounded by experts who might know all about multimedia, CD-ROMs, the internet, virtual reality etc. in both business and home settings, make up your own exciting new area. Any combination of plausible words will do: 'edutainment', 'cybertracking', 'multi-dimensional virtuality', that sort of thing. All current areas will be obsolete within five years because of the new technology you've just made up, and the distinction between home and business computing will be meaningless.

2. The **"Oh still using that one!"** put-down.

Always sneer at every piece of software used by other people. Whatever they admit to using – whether it be word processor, game, or interactive singing and dancing multimedia encyclopædia of all human knowledge – it is already out of date. The new version, shortly to be launched in the United States, is faster, much more powerful, has superior graphics, and comes on a CD-ROM. If theirs is already a CD-ROM, the new version comes on two. Of course the new one costs twice as much; but there is a public domain (i.e. free) program which does everything the version they have does, so they have wasted their money. You can't remember its name, but it is available on the Internet. This is always true for any piece of software, so you can safely say it at any time.

3. The **"For my next trick"** trick.

Here, you need to insinuate that not only is the other person's area of computing interest and software obsolete, but their computer is totally outdated too. The computer industry is the only one in the world to suffer from rampant deflation. Prices of hardware drop even faster than the rate at which they are superseded.

So, whatever they have, say it is now half the price they paid because it is shortly to be replaced by a faster, bigger, cheaper one. If theirs was a 486, the new model is a 586, and so on. It does not matter what these figures mean, nor if you know or care. It is just that 686 is clearly better than 586, which is obviously superior to 486, and 386 is self-evidently Jurassic. Similarly, if they have a pokey 500 megabyte hard drive, the new one has a more spacious 2000 megabyte hard drive. It has cinemascope, quadrophonic sound, Wurlitzer organ and satellite dish. Make up anything; it is bound to be on somebody's R and D schedule.

If anyone dares to admit they have never heard of it,

say IBM have still got it under wraps in this country, but that they are launching it at an office equipment show in Anaheim (L.A.). No-one will disbelieve that.

4. The **"I wouldn't dirty my hands"** opening.

Never admit to using a computer for any practical reason. Never mention using databases, games or worst of all, a word processor. The real computer bluffer should only have a computer for some peculiarly esoteric purpose to do with programming, particularly if it can only be done by accessing data over the phone lines from an obscure American university. To admit you gain some commercial advantage from your computer is like an avant-garde poet admitting that he writes greetings-card verse.

5. The **"It needs a bit of tweaking"** gambit.

Never admit to using a commercial program. Whatever purpose you use your computer for, say you use a wonderfully powerful Public Domain program that you downloaded free over the phone from America, although you would not recommend everyone to use it because it takes a bit of 'tweaking' to get it to run.

Tweaking means taking someone else's program, usually written for a slightly different purpose or machine, and improving it or adapting it to work on your own. Anyone with any pretensions to being a computer buff has a house full of PD programs that they can't get to work; programs bought on the recommendation of a friend who mentioned that "all it needs is a little tweaking".

You can make up any reasonable-sounding name for your PD program and recommend it: 'QuickWord' for example ("a nice compact word processor, but needs a tweak to work on newer PCs", you might say) or 'EasyDraw 5' ("does everything Adobe Photoshop does and more, but needs tweaking to work on modern laser printers"). People will never attempt to buy the non-existent program you have recommended, though they might recommend it to someone else. If you are really lucky, you could one day find your spurious program recommended to you – although "it might need a bit of tweaking". If this happens you can regard yourself as a master bluffer.

6. The **"I believe they used to load programs with tape recorders"** scam.

It is a rule throughout the computer industry that you should be young. Very young. There is no point boasting at age 30 that you have learned how to set the tab stops on your word processor. Within minutes you will be confronted by a nine-year-old who has been writing his own word processor program in C. It is simpler to keep dyeing your hair and pretending you cannot remember a time before CD-ROMs.

Deprecate others' experience. Anything learnt ten days ago is liable to be out of date. Anything learnt ten years ago is as useful as a technique for hunting a sabre-toothed tiger with a flint-tipped spear; besides, there is now a PD program that can do that for you.

7. The **"IBM is a fully instituted TLA"** fol-de-rol.

The most important concept for a successful computer bluffer is the **TLA**. It is the only thing common throughout computing from games machine to mainframe. It stands, of course, for the Three Letter Abbreviation: CPU, LCD, ROM etc. etc.

How the TLA was invented is lost in the mists of antiquity. It has been suggested that three letters were chosen because of the well-known fact that computers can only count up to two (see Computers and Numbers) and this was proof of human superiority.

The TLA is not used for convenience. Try saying 'VDU' and then 'screen' and decide which is easier. The real reasons for the TLA are:

a) to cause confusion
b) to be purposely obscure
c) to let you feel smug, much as lawyers use Latin.

Use the TLA mercilessly. Not 'processor', but CPU; not 'display', but LCD; not 'memory', but RAM. Carry it off with confidence and no-one will ask you what the letters stand for. The only areas to avoid are ones that are so well known that everyone thinks they know what they mean (IBM, VAT, BMW etc.). Once you are sure that you are not clashing with a real TLA the rest of the alphabet is yours to play with (you would need a computer to work out the number of permutations). A good computer bluffer will take the NNB (Number Nine Bus) to his POE (Place of Employment) after a good breakfast of MNX (memory nodule extensions).

Computers and the Public

The general public labours under several misconceptions about computers. One of these is that computers are there to save human labour.

In fact, the reverse is true. Their specific purpose is to create more of it. As more and more people are made unemployed because they have been replaced by a single microchip, they have to have something to fill their time.

This is why every piece of electronic equipment in the world has a computer installed: photocopiers, videos, microwave ovens, wedding greetings cards that play the theme from *Kramer versus Kramer* when you open them, etc. Without a computer installed, you would just press a single red button to photocopy a single sheet of A4, for example. With it you only have to press 19 buttons in a precise sequence, playing a tune like the *Close Encounters* theme, to find yourself printing 100 copies at one per cent the size of the original.

Personal computers are the same. They are made more and more difficult to use every year in order to soak up all that time freed up by personal computers. The average piece of software now takes about two years to learn – by which time a new, completely different, version has come out.

Computer Manuals

Everyone knows the First Law of Micro-Processing: 'If all else fails, Read The Manual'.* A true bluffer would never make such an irresponsible statement. This

* (This has its own TLA of course: RTM. There is a four-letter variant, RTFM, to be used with care.)

document is a vital element in a bluff that has kept the general public out of computers for years.

If you ever are faced with the unthinkable – actually having to get a piece of software to work – the way to tackle it is by playing about with the program and finding out by trial and error what it does. Once you have mastered the program it is relatively easy to go back to the manual and work out what it means. This might take some time, so send out no dinner invitations for the next two weeks. Particularly if you were intending to write them out on a computer.

If anyone else needs to use the software, insist they start by reading the manual from cover to cover. Say something like, "You'll find the appendix on networking with non-DOS machines invaluable."

It doesn't matter if you don't understand any of that. It doesn't matter if there aren't any appendices. They won't get that far. They will still be ploughing their way through helpful pieces of information like *'the syntax for this command is DEVICE logical-device1 = physical-device1, physical device2, [physical-deviceN]'* or *'Designated drive: ambiguous filename: argument'*.

Reading the average computer manual, you realise that the industry has been infiltrated at the highest levels by world-class bluffers. If others believe you understand them, your reputation is assured forever.

Error Messages

Have a plentiful supply of these phrases that appear on the screen to announce something has gone wrong and you have just lost all your work for the last month.

There is a game amongst computer programmers to

see who can produce the longest and most obscure error message in the world. One strong contender that appeared on a mainframe computer was the message *'VME ERROR 37022: Hierarchic name syntax invalid taking into account starting points defined by initial context.'* That's a real one.

The mark of a good program is not its user-friendliness but the originality and creativity or its error messages. Once you realise it is all a game, you can face *'Unexpected diagnostic verification violation'* flashing on your screen with total equanimity.

Where error messages come in really useful is when you reach that dreadful moment: you are asked to do something on the computer you don't know how to do. A normal person would stupidly blurt out something like "I don't know how to do that." But the bluffer just smiles quietly, confidently presses a few significant-looking keys, stares at the screen with a worried expression – and, when nothing happens, murmurs, "Oh dear. Looks like we've got severe mantissa buffering overload in the high addresses."

Strictly speaking, this does not mean anything. But no-one ever asks what it does mean. Let the other person decide whether you should go on, once you have been warned that there is an *'Untrapped Illegal Stack Deficiency in 720.'*

Here are three useful error messages you can use, with a short explanation of what they mean.

'Severe retrieval format corruption' – nothing.
'Non-recoverable global drivespec mixing in 4070' – nothing.
'Terminal high byte consolidation violation' – nothing.

Computers and Numbers

The main thing you need to remember about computers and numbers is that you can totally confuse the average listener even if you have no mathematical ability yourself. If anyone questions you on numbers just remind them that computers can only add up to one (starting at zero, of course). These are called **binary numbers** and are of no practical use to anyone using a computer. The main purpose of binary is to confuse your audience so they will not see the gaping holes in the reasoning of later discussions.

The other thing to remember is that the most important use of numbers are those used in the name of your computer. These are always so vague even the makers are not sure why they chose them so you can use any combination of numbers with little fear of being caught out. If you have made up a computer for yourself always add a number – the Doppelganger ZQ768, for instance.

If more mathematically capable, you could use any number divisible by 256 – the computer's mystical number. That must be worth something.

Hex

If any listeners look as if they are beginning to grasp the idea of binary, slip into a lecture on **hex** numbers without any explanation. In the hexadecimal system a computer doesn't just count up to one. It counts up to 16, but calls it 10. (Please note that no matter how clever computers are supposed to be, they never seem to have caught on to the fact that everyone else counts up to ten.)

As 16 single digits are not available you have to use letters as numbers in hex: 0B, for example, represents 'eleven' and 3F is 'sixty-three'. So remember that when you quote a hex figure it will always have two digits, one or both of which could be a letter between A and F. The major advantage of counting in hex, however, is that at your fortieth birthday you can truthfully tell the world you are 28.

ASCII

Should a particularly bright listener show the slightest potential to grasp the idea of hex, skip to the fact that computers treat letters (in, say, a text document) as numbers. The secret is hidden in the snappily-titled American Standard Code for Information Interchange, (ASCII), pronounced 'As-key'.

As codes go, this one is childishly easy to break: in it '?' is 63, 'A' is 65, 'B' is 66 and so on. Even so-called word processors work like this, turning all letters into numbers, which are then turned into ones and zeros for binary, which are in turn translated into hex numbers, consisting of letters and numbers. Of course, some trivial symbols are not covered by the code and cannot be put into such documents – such as the rarely-used '£' symbol, for instance.

By now you should have lost your listener completely, especially if your text document was 'a letter' to start with.

The idea is that if you have a file translated into ASCII code, it can be read by virtually any computer. What they don't tell you is that if you have an ASCII file on a CD-ROM, you can't get it into a 3½" disc drive.

WHICH COMPUTER?

You have to decide which computer to be an expert on. Here is a run-down of the main types; pick one to suit your image.

Mainframes

Mainframes are the big, impressive business computers that add ICI's electricity bill to yours. They fill several air-conditioned rooms but do not look like computers in films – the ones with 15,000 red lights that flash on and off constantly and make strange buzzing noises. This is largely because no-one has yet thought up any purpose for the 15,000 flashing lights and even ICI could not afford the electricity bill.

It is not a good idea to bluff about mainframes. They cost so much that only insurance companies, banks and recently privatised industries can afford them. It is hard to be thought interesting when claiming to be in charge of computing Social Security payments for the whole of the West of Scotland.

There are only one or two areas of mainframe computing that could be regarded as even vaguely romantic:

1. The first is AI (**Artificial Intelligence**, not Artificial Insemination – do not try to impress a farmer by saying you are in AI or he will ask you to do things that turn your hair grey).

Originally AI was the theory that a computer could be developed that would effectively mimic human intelligence, and develop its own identity and awareness.

Quite why anyone would want to build a computer that would probably demand overtime pay for weekend work is not known. The general belief is that the idea originated with computer programmers, desperate to have someone to talk to who would not find them boring.

2. The other is the military, who have World War III already on disc. The computers will launch the missiles, aim the guns, plan the strategy, polish the boots and play the bugle first thing in the morning. All they need is a soldier bright enough to understand the manual.

Terminals

The next stage down from having a mainframe to play with is to have a 'terminal' (a screen and a keyboard which are connected to a mainframe – nothing to do with a serious illness). This can give a real feeling of power, knowing that you are tying up part of a multi-million pound computer while typing a letter to your mother using two fingers.

Apart from this they are not much fun. You can get all the specialist software to buy and sell shares at the stock exchange, and that sort of thing, but they are usually dreadfully short of good adventure games and virtually none have anywhere to attach a joystick.

The best examples are the systems they have for laying out the pages in the bright, new, full-colour, all-action tabloid newspapers. Some have now gone to the length of putting everything, including the air conditioning, on to the same computer – so when anyone switches on the central heating, the computer mis-spells every other name on the front page. This is a real technological advance. Until now it took ten reporters and four sub-editors to mis-spell every other name on the front page.

Desktops

Desktops are so named, not because you can write on them but because they sit on your desk (quite often that is all they do). They used to be called Micros since they were smaller than the manuals that came with them.

They are essential purchases, especially for the self-employed or those in small businesses, not because they save time or effort – they waste them – but because they are tax-deductible ways of playing games.

Laptops or Portables

Portables have developed into a significant part of the computer market. This is not because your portable allows you to take your work with you on holiday or to your home. It's because you can use it on the train.

People don't interrupt you from your work to ask questions about processors or spreadsheets. They just ask, "What are you doing?" The answer is obvious. As with a mobile phone, there is only one thing you can be doing using a computer on a crowded train – you are showing off.

PERSONAL COMPUTERS

The personal computer is the main area for computer bluffing. First, do you spell it 'disks' or 'discs'?

Discs (or Disks)

The storage medium for all data on personal computers, and the longest-standing and most contentious controversy: should you spell it the 'English' or 'American' way? Whichever the other person uses, say it should be the other, and make up any plausible reason ("Bill Gates himself has said it should be 'disk'/'disc',") to back up your case.

Disks (or discs) are strange creatures. They vary in shape from little flat plastic things the size of a beer mat to massive electric-powered boxes the size of a beer tray. Anything that is not a massive box is called a floppy disc (or disk) despite the fact that it is neither round nor floppy, and the big boxes are called hard disks because they are easy. Floppies can be slipped in your pocket, although trying to do this with a hard drive could give you a slipped disc (or disk).

Should you spill the beer glass you have rested on a floppy, you will destroy around one megabyte of data – about enough to store a telephone directory. If you spill the tray of beer over your hard disk, you will destroy the company's financial records for the last three years.

Floppies used to come in the sort of standard size you would expect in a hi-tech modern industry – 3", 3½", 5¼", 8", then, just as the 3½" became the norm, onto the scene came 5" compact discs (or disks). This is all part of the computer industry's aim of achieving one standard of incompatibility.

19

Which PC?

The next step is: which make and model of personal computer should you buy?

The answer is simple: none. This will save you the worry of knowing that your machine will be obsolete in three months, and will save you hours of time in the manuals you don't have to read. It will also make it easier to be superior to people at parties, who will tell you enthusiastically which machine they have. Here's how to bluff them into feeling good or, more amusingly, that they have bought the wrong model.

IBM Compatible PC

The IBM Personal Computer (which is what people usually have in mind when they talk about 'PCs') quickly established itself as the standard machine for home and business use for no good reason other than that it had become the standard machine. Other companies brought out 'clones', i.e. machines identical in every respect except the price, which was much lower.

IBM makes everything optional. Even the keyboard, without which it is clearly impossible to operate the machine, is 'optional'. It is said that in IBM's canteens, lunch is only $4 – plus $2 each for the optional plate, knife and fork.

There are innumerable manufacturers, mostly Far Eastern, constantly bringing out faster and cheaper models. So, get the other person to outline their own machine's specifications and price, and then make up an oriental-sounding 'PC' you know about: "Have you seen the new Sukiyaki/Dim Sum/Wan Ton? Everything your machine does, for £500 less. Don't know *how* they do it..."

Good point: Every program that has ever been written comes out in a form you can use on the PC so you have the choice of all the best programs for everything.

Bad point: To know what program to buy from the bewildering choice of the tens of thousands available, you have to buy a magazine to help you. These are the size and weight of a paving slab, and just as attractive and readable. However, all come with free cover-mounted discs, which make good beer mats.

Apple Macintosh

The Mac's claim to fame is that it is so simple to use even designers and journalists can cope with it. It is termed 'friendly' (although still not a great conversationalist) because of its pictorial way of working: to erase a file for example, you move the icon representing it into a little picture of a wastebasket, and so on. (The PC version of this is called Windows, because it is transparently the same idea.) Macs have been overtaken by PCs in sales, however, because Apple would not let Sukiyaki, Dim Sum etc. make clones of the Macintosh. To show their commitment to this principle they have recently brought out their top-of-the-range 'Power Macs' which are, in fact, IBM PC clones.

Good points: Very friendly and easy to use, with all errors explained to you. Huge range of software, especially graphics. Thanks to belated price drops, now affordable to non-professionals.

Bad point: Like all computers it has error messages, but in an irritatingly laid-back West-Coast-of-America way: if a document cannot print out, instead of saying the usual 'Printer error #7633: irretrievable PostScript version mismatch', it will say 'Hi! Hey, I'm really sorry about this, but I've crashed. The document was OK. I just can't print it out right now.'

Amstrad PCW

Marketed by Alan Sugar's Amstrad plc as a word processor, complete with printer and word processing software. Millions have been sold, mostly in the UK to people who don't even know that what they have is a computer. Owners of PCWs are usually very proud of the fact that they don't know how to do anything with their computer except type letters.

Good point: Cheap and great for word processing.

Bad point: No good for anything else. Other computers can play music, for example; the PCW can only beep a B flat, restricting its repertoire to *One Note Samba*, and then in the wrong key. And the now obsolete 3" discs make rotten beer mats.

Spectrum/CPC/Commodore

The good old cheap games machines, now superseded by Sega and Nintendo consoles.

Good point: Just the basic, no-nonsense, unpretentious sort of computers no-one would be ashamed to start on.

Bad point: Just the basic, no-nonsense, unpretentious sort of computers no-one would admit to having now.

Amiga and Atari ST

Great rivals in the late 1980s for the serious games player's money, a battle Amiga won. Amiga magazines are the ones with two or three free discs on the cover, because Amiga owners drink more beer.

Good points: The vast potential for graphic design and animation, and for making electronic music, is limited only by the user's talent and imagination.

Bad points: Most of the aspiring graphic designers, animators and musicians using them have no talent or imagination.

Games Consoles: Sega, Nintendo etc.

Games consoles have been exploding – every three seconds, in the nasty violent games they run. Their current popularity with games players is a form of reverse snobbery: they would not sully their hands on a machine so sordid it can add things up or help to write a letter. Or more likely, games console owners have no-one to write a letter to, or anything to add up, and therefore do not require a machine that can do this.

Good points: None.

Bad point: The magazines run from cartridges, not discs, and so consoles magazines cannot cover-mount anything to rest your beer glass on.

COMPUTERS IN THE WORLD

Computers are evident in all facets of life, so whatever the subject under discussion, computers will be involved – and the person you are talking to will have something to say about them. Therefore you should know just enough about their subject to disparage what they say, and enough about any other subject to convince them that it is much more interesting, useful and relevant than theirs.

The Internet

Everyone has heard the word Internet (or just Net), but few know what it means, so explain it as the electronic equivalent of a world road system. A road by itself is only useful because of what it links you to: your friends' houses, the shops, libraries, pubs, etc. You can use the road system usefully – to visit these buildings – or just wander up and down aimlessly. Similarly, the Internet can be useful – you can visit friends, shops, libraries and communal meeting-places from your screen – or you just wander aimlessly up and down the network – 'netsurfing'.

The 'road sign' system is the World Wide Web, a system which ensures that the information from one computer will be displayed in a legible way on any other on the Internet (if the message comes across as unreadable rubbish, then it really is unreadable rubbish). It also provides a framework to guide you round the Net, as road signs are meant to do.

In theory by 2010 (or any similar date: make one up) everyone will be on the Internet, and everyone will be able to look up train times, book a theatre ticket or flight, order groceries, talk to friends, download software for their computers, hear the latest CDs, see the latest films, work on their office computer etc., all from home. A splendid way of keeping computer users off the streets.

Electronic Mail (e-mail)

The ability to send messages, screen to screen, to anyone else on the Internet, with special mail programs you buy. Everyone has a unique address, based on the sort of computing institution they are connected to, e.g. John Smith at the University of Edinburgh might be jsmith@edinburgh.ac.uk – enough to have any electronic mail in the world find him. The usual format of the first bit is initial-surname, so speculate on the embarrassment caused for people with names like Tim Watt, or Paul Anka's brother William.

The advantages of e-mail are obvious: the accessibility and instantaneous nature of communication (it takes as long to send something to Tottenham as to Tokyo) meaning you can send messages to any other computer at the touch of a button. The disadvantages are also obvious for the same reasons – you can easily find your e-mail box full of hundreds of messages daily from people who wouldn't have dreamt of writing to you.

The amount of repeated typing involved in e-mail have led to plenty of bizarre acronyms – not just TLAs but ETLAs (Extended Three-Letter Abbreviations, i.e. more than three). BTW is 'By The Way'; ROFL is 'Rolls On Floor Laughing' (given the standard of humour on the Internet, it is difficult to see why this has evolved); BCNU is 'Be Seeing You'; FOAD is – well, the last two words are 'And Die', which shows the imagination involved in most 'flaming' (sending angry messages).

Even more bizarre is the use of **smileys**, or **emoticons** as the Americans call them. Because e-mailers are never sure about the tone of a written message (jocular? serious? tongue-in-cheek? angry? sarcastic?) they often add combinations of characters which represent a facial expression to show the tone of the message. The expression becomes clear when the page is turned sideways:

:-) basic smiley
;-) winking smiley
:-(sad smiley
>:-> devilish smiley
B-) wears horn-rimmed glasses
R-) wears broken horn-rimmed glasses
*<R-O wears broken horn-rimmed glasses and a Santa Claus hat, and is yawning.

Newsgroups

Newsgroups are public forums devoted to a particular subject. You could access things like your favourite rock band's newsgroup, to read the latest news, correspond using e-mail with other fans, read dates of their gigs, perhaps download to your own computer and then play an extract of their latest recording.

A favourite subject for newsgroups is of course pornography. Make up any weird fetishist group with a name such as 'alt dot sex dot footfetish' (which is a real one) and invent things about it. Use this to either defend or attack the concept of the Internet.

Everything Else

The Internet is so disorganised and scattered that anything is possible, so whatever claim you make about what you have been able to access will be true, if not now, then by the year 2010.

Virtual Reality

This is more worlds-in-the-computer than computers-in-the-world. The idea is that a computer-generated representation of something – a fantasy game world or a new building design, say – can be so detailed it feels real. It does this by being able to alter your viewpoint so you can 'wander round' it. The usual way is that you don a headset with a screen for each eye. As you turn your head, the scene changes to make it seem you are actually inside the world or building.

You must denigrate virtual reality ("unconvincing graphics... jerky animations... processing power not up to it for another hundred years... cases of induced seizures in virtual reality testers", etc., even though it is not true) and say it is only a frivolous cul-de-sac in computing development, devised purely for architects to plump up their budgets and make their powerful games computers tax-deductible. Unless you *are* an architect, in which case virtual reality is an exciting new field with huge potential to save millions of pounds.

Computers in the Office

This is the most obvious place where a computer might be useful, so you should tread warily. However, there are niches for highly-paid careers in computer bluffing.

Everything depends on finding the right boss. The ideal is someone in their 50s who feels that computers are a "good idea" and will make the company "more efficient", but still has only the vaguest idea what they do.

Better still you might find the rare breed who proudly announce they "know nothing about computers" in the same way they would tell you there is definitely no mental illness in their family. In fact, to them, an ability to understand computers is a definite sign of a warped mind. You can go far in a company like this.

The best situation is to join the company just after it has spent thousands of pounds on one of those specialised software packages that never works. Someone has to take the blame for having spent thousands of pounds on a product that is useless, so there is usually a vacancy for a Systems Manager about six weeks after the software is installed.

Do not rush to get the software working. This would spoil all the fun and would mean that the managing director has nothing to moan about at the golf club on Sunday afternoons.

You must quickly concede that it just will not work "in its present form", but you could perhaps get it to work "with a bit of tweaking".

Naturally you do not actually do anything to the program but if it suddenly starts working in some form or other, they think you are the only person in the world who really knows how it works now, and you are suddenly indispensable.

Technical Queries

Once you are indispensable, your 'detailed' knowledge of computers may lead someone to ask you a technical question. Never be worried about these; the fact that they ask means they would not understand the answer anyway. If someone starts talking about chips and processors and bus boards, direct them to an electronic engineer (or a café or London Transport timetable, as suitable).

Questions you will be asked are of three types:

a) Is there any way I can print out sideways on my word processor?

b) I'm running Megabase IV version 3 under Windows version 3.6.4.17 and there seems to be a glitch which resets the defaults by overwriting four bytes of RAM when I run a batch file. How can I get round this?

c) My computer won't work, what's wrong with it?

The techniques to adopt are:

1. First ask if the computer has a Pentium processor. If the answer is yes, say that the software is not backwardly compatible with that processor. If the answer is no, say that is what the problem is – what is required can only be done on a Pentium. If the individual does not know, go to step 2.

2. Listen intently and ask what version of the program it is and where they live. Then say, "Ahhh, there were problems with that version in the Wolverhampton area" (or wherever). If pressed, go to step 3.

3. Go deep into thought for a few seconds then pick one of the following:

a) "Yes, you can do it, but it's very difficult unless you're familiar with C." (Nobody asking will know C, so no problem here.)

b) "There's a program in the public domain which will do it for you with a bit of tweaking, I've forgotten the name, but it's something like V-G8/W_O.EXE." (This is always true.)

c) "I recall that there's a bug on that version which has been fixed in the latest version. Unfortunately it costs £2,500 more." (Again, this is always true, so you are safe here too.)

If all else fails, remember the one sure-fire cure for computer problems which never fails to impress when it works, and which actually works in 99 per cent of cases: switch the machine off and then on again. NB: this is not advisable with a mainframe.

Computers in the Home

Educational Software

This is a boom industry which depends upon parents convincing themselves they have not bought little Johnny a computer just so that he can blat little green men from the planet Zog.

It means that they will fork out for a succession of rather unlikely programs with tantalising titles like *Advanced Calculus Can be Fun* – proof that the Trades Descriptions Act does not apply to software.

Most educational programs are no more than a plausible-looking opening screen. Few people ever run them right through to see if they do what they are supposed to do (especially the children they were intended for).

This is therefore the easiest field for the programming bluffer. You could quickly learn enough BASIC to knock up an opening screen and four pages of really dreary questions (about two more pages than are really required) and call it *Paddington Bear's Quadratic Equation Game*. This brings it into line with most proprietary software where the real creative effort goes into writing the blurb on the disc cover.

The best educational programs usually involve dull sums or complicated words to spell. There is always a little animated figure that jumps up and down if you get it right or shakes his head and makes a noise that sounds something like 'oh-oh' if you get it wrong. The person who comes up with the hardware to allow the computer to give little Johnny an electric shock if he got it wrong would probably retire early and rich.

Home Accounts Packages

The most unlikely thing to use a personal computer for is to look after home finances. No one realises this – until they have invested in a package. The sign of an expert bluffer is when you can get people to part with a £100 in the belief that it will save them money.

As the people who buy this sort of program are those who always read the manual, if the documentation is daunting enough you could almost risk selling them a blank disc. There is little chance that they will use the program twice. Few occupations are more soul-destroying than spending an evening finding out exactly how much money you have squandered this week and projecting how much of an overdraft you will have next week.

Multimedia

Multimedia is the concept of mixing high-quality sound, graphics, video and text on a single machine. Computers that can run multimedia programs have the latest technology sound cards and high-resolution screens. They can also read CD-ROMs, the only things with a big enough storage capacity to hold graphics, videos and sound.

All these perform an important function. They allow you to look things up in an encyclopædia. There was a time when people hid if an encyclopædia salesman called at the door. Nowadays they spend a fortune to have an encyclopædia on compact disc.

Of course the computerised encyclopædia is far better than the old version. When you look up the word 'llama' it shows you a 30-second video of a llama with a backing track of muzak and an American voiceover that says 'the llama is a beast of burden, common in South America'.

This is clearly an invaluable aid to learning, as the voiceover, music, video and accompanying text can be cut out and pasted straight into the multimedia essay on llamas being prepared by the child on the same computer. Before multimedia, the child would have to read and understand the six-paragraph encyclopædia entry, and then write it up manually, which is clearly no way to gain an education.

Computers in Schools

Do not get involved with anything to do with computers in schools. There is absolutely no money in it and without fail all the kids will know more about the computers than you or the teachers do.

COMPUTER USER TYPES

Just as the Chinese all look alike to the Westerner, computer people can all look alike to an inexperienced bluffer. However, with a little practice you should be able to tell them apart and make use of this information.

Here is a short run-down of the major groups with 'tell-tale signs' that will enable you to pick them out.

Programmers

There are two types of people who write programs. The first write boring specialist accounts programs for companies. They have neat new company cars and have to be smart for their job, even though they never meet anybody while doing it. They hate their jobs.

The second group write games and multimedia software, freelance, at home. They wear sweatshirts and John Lennon glasses, and have long hair and pot bellies. They spend all their money on beer, and have huge collections of beer mats which are actually the free cover discs of computer magazines. They love their jobs.

Neither type ever talks about the programs they are writing so it is easy to pass yourself off as one.

Tell-tale signs: Strange sense of humour – they laugh at nothing except non-sequiturs. This is because misuse of logic reminds them of the programs they write. They use 'k' to mean 'thousand', as in 'I hear they're offering him 36k plus company car'.

When to pretend to be a software writer: When in the company of games programmers, who will buy you lots of beer.

Mistakes to avoid in conversation: Type 1: Asking why they hate their job. Type 2: Asking why they love their job.

I've-Computerised-My-Business Types

These people have bought one or two cheap computers in the vague hope that they will 'streamline things', 'get ahead' and 'save money in the long run'. They end up having to pay for expensive maintenance contracts in case the things go wrong; they send their staff on costly computer training courses every month at several hundred pounds per person per day; and they get several months behind as they learn how to use them. The only benefit is that they can now blame every mistake on 'computer error' to credulous customers.

Never believe any nonsense they tell you about the 'paperless office' (the idea that all your paperwork can be stored on disc instead of paper). Point out that using a computer necessitates:

- boxes of continuous paper next to the printer
- manuals for the software you use
- books telling you how to actually use the software because the manual is a literal translation from the Japanese
- waste paper bins for the paper that is wasted when the machine prints 2,000 copies of a letter dated February 30th 1067
- boxes of discs
- boxes of backup discs for emergency copies of data
- print-outs of all the documents which have been put on disc anyway.

Tell-tale signs: Inky fingers from having changed the printer ribbon four times during their print run of 2,000 customer letters. Haggard, tired expression. Dogged belief that it will all come right in the end. Irrational trust in new technology.

When to pretend to be a computerised business person: When trying to convince your customers that the wrong invoice you sent was 'computer error'.

Mistakes to avoid in conversation: "Tell me, how do you handle your accounts?"

Dedicated Word Processors

Everyone is aware that a monkey hitting a typewriter at random will produce the entire works of Shakespeare if you wait long enough – say the end of eternity, or until someone writes a software manual in plain English, whichever is the longer. Since the invention of the word processor, this can be done much more quickly, and a large number of monkeys have already started on the mammoth task – disguised as a group of people called 'dedicated word processors'.

These are a strange breed, largely because they may not even know that they own a computer. They are often married women with growing children who have bought it to write books for Mills and Boon rather than allow their brains to atrophy. Or retired colonels who live under the strange delusion that people will be interested in knowing what they did in the war, who also end up writing for Mills and Boon.

There is no use trying to bluff these people with

technical terms. They know none and are completely unperturbed if you point out this fact to them. To this breed, 'getting technical' means finding out how to set tabs on a page.

Yet without fail they will be able to tell you how it is possible to use the FIND/EXCHANGE facility to change every occurrence of the name David in a 100,000 word novel to the name Dick at a single stroke – thus producing an inadvert reference to the famous sculpture, Michelangelo's Dick.

Tell-tale signs: Publishers' rejection slips sticking out of every pocket. Wide-eyed expression.

When to pretend to be a dedicated word processor: Only when you meet an attractive member of the opposite sex who has some literary pretensions. It combines the attractions of knowledge of computers with a creative streak.

Mistakes to avoid in conversation: Letting them tell you every detail of the plot development in their four volume blockbusting novel about passion and intrigue amongst the train spotters of West Penge.

Hackers

Hacking – breaking into programs or computers and viewing or altering information illicitly – sounds as if it should be exciting. It isn't, except during the trial.

There are two types of hackers:

Type 1. Lone back-bedroom geniuses, with chips on both

shoulders and a grudge against humanity, who use their computer to hack into the Pentagon's computer system through the phone line in order to gain access to America's defence secrets.

This type was a staple ingredient of 1980s sci-fi films in which there was a remarkable graphics compatibility. Once accessed, the Pentagon's World War III software designed to run on a multi-billion dollar computer magically ran on the hacker's hundred-buck machine, with high-quality graphics working perfectly on his portable TV screen. The hackers also typed at 120wpm without ever making mistakes.

Gaining access to other people's computers is surprisingly easy. It usually involves simply guessing and typing a password, and there you are, reading Prince Philip's computer mailbox (as once notoriously happened). Computer users choose imaginative passwords such as PASSWORD (so obvious no-one would ever guess it) QWERTY or FRED (easy to type on a keyboard), names of their family members, or characters from the only books they have read (invariably the *Hitch-Hiker's Guide to the Galaxy*, *Lord of the Rings* or William Gibson's 'cyberpunk' novels). These are, of course, the first things a hacker tries, usually with instant success.

Type 2. Lone back-bedroom teenagers, with spots on both shoulders and a grudge against parents, who spend years of their lives reading and amending machine code of games programs.

This is a tedious job, as it involves screen after screen of numbers with a few letters thrown in. The object is to change the way the games work to make them easier –

by slowing down the opposition, increasing your ammunition and so on. Such amendments are called 'pokes'. It is obvious that these are lonely people, lacking in social graces, for they believe it is possible to talk about 'pokes' in polite society and get away with it.

Tell-tale signs: Type 1: You never meet them, but when you turn on your computer, you find Prince Philip's mail in your 'letters' folder and details of World War III in your 'household expenses' file. Type 2: An ability to say "I've got a great poke for Jet Set Willy" without seeing anything funny in it.

Mistakes to avoid in conversation: Type 1: "You'll never guess my password." Type 2: "Hello."

Netsurfers

These are the people who roam around the Internet – the network of business and personal computers interconnected over phone lines (the 'information superhighway').

Because their only contact with people is screen to screen, they like taking on other guises; almost all those 'erotic women' contributing to the sexual forums accessible on the Internet are teenage boys pretending to be women, and almost all the 'erotic men' replying to them are other teenage boys.

And, because they only ever contact other netsurfers, their language involves heavy use of jargon and metaphors as mixed-up as the teenage boys pretending to be women. They are wired, on-line 'infonauts', surfing the 'infobahn' while 'flaming newbies' (sending angry messages to new Net users).

They like extolling the virtues of world access from your computer screen: you can, for example, order goods and services from there without having to go out into the real world. This is clearly a very good thing – for the real world.

Tell-tale signs: Try to talk about the 'communications revolution' but prefer to go home and send a message from their computer screen to yours – when their inability to communicate really does start to show.

Mistakes to avoid in conversation: "I beg your pardon, could you explain 'access alt dot sex dot footfetish' on the Usenet for me?" But conversation can usually be totally avoided by not buying a modem.

When to pretend to be a netsurfer: When you want to get rid of a netsurfer who is talking to you. They will ask for your e-mail address (make one up: see next section) and immediately race home to continue the conversation screen-to-screen.

Games Players

Games players are people who wear T-shirts and jeans and sit inside on sunny summer evenings in their bedrooms playing adventure games or killing aliens. They have an encyclopædic knowledge of every screen on every game they have played. They get into vehement arguments with other games players about whether the most difficult level in Lemmings was the fifth or the sixth, and whether Doom was overrated.

There are two types of games players:

Type 1. Ostensibly normal people with responsible jobs who only become games players in the evenings and are ashamed to tell anyone of their inclinations.

Type 2. Adolescent boys whose bedrooms are full of games and games magazines to which they write hopelessly ungrammatical and badly spelt letters on lined notepaper consisting entirely of the words brill, fab, wow, cool, mega and great, and sign themselves 'Mr' thinking this will convince somebody they are over 21.

Tell-tale signs: A trembling of the thumb while talking to you as they subconsciously work the joystick on level 6 of Sonic the Hedgehog. Plastic bags with budget game-and-magazine-size bulges in them. Baseball caps. Abnormally high use of the words 'brill', 'fab', 'level', 'poke' and 'pixel' in conversation. Spots.

When to pretend to be a games player: When you need to establish good relations with adolescents.

Mistakes to avoid in conversation: Talking about high scores.

APPLICATIONS

'Applications' is just another word for 'programs' though it sounds better. A computer is useless without programs to run. The programs you buy depend on what you want to use it for, so here is a list of the types of program and what they can do. Of course it is not for your own purposes, it is for those occasions when you talk to someone who has just bought a piece of software. Using the following list, you will be able to convince them that they bought wrongly and have made an expensive mistake.

Any program with pretensions has spurious capitals in the middle of the word – MegaBase, WonderCalc and so on. It all arose from the early days of programming, when names of things in programs couldn't have spaces. To make clear where the break in words was, a capital letter was used, the classic examples being two frequently-used graphics variables: PenIsUp and PenIsDown.

Word Processors

Instead of using a clanky old typewriter, the idea is you type documents into your computer which stores the text on disc. You can edit bits of the text, format it as you like, reset the line spacing, move paragraphs around etc. as you wish. You only print it out when you are satisfied the document is perfect. It is shortly after printing and switching off you notice you have spelt your own name wrong.

Typical programs: Microsoft Word, WordPerfect, LocoScript.

Disadvantages: Documents fall into two types: (a) quick letters and memos and, (b) longer documents where presentation is all-important such as business reports and newsletters.

Clearly it is more trouble than it is worth with (a) to start up your computer, load the operating system, load the word processor, type in your letter, check it, print it out, print it out again because the first one was too far to the left in the printer, and save it to disc just to say 'Two extra pints please, Mr Milkman'. What you need, you say, is a pen which is roughly £1,000 cheaper.

With (b), word processors are just not powerful enough to cope with the functions you need – text in variously positioned boxes, footnotes, graphs and high-quality picture handling, etc. What you really should be using, you tell them, is a desktop publisher.

Desktop Publishers

'DTP' programs let you manipulate text into columns and boxes, include graphics and high-quality photos directly in the document, and then place it all anywhere you like on a page to get the best arrangement before printing out or turning it into film to send to the printers. This is used for books, newsletters, posters, flyers, magazines and so on, and it is always obvious which feature of the program the designer has just discovered how to use. It is shortly after printing and switching off you notice you have spelt the title wrong.

Typical programs: Aldus PageMaker, Quark XPress.

Disadvantages: To match the range of devices and

quality of output you can get from traditional typesetting-plus-paste-up (multiple overlays, graduated tints etc.) DTP programs have to be very big, very powerful and very expensive. But mostly you want headlines and column text with some high-quality pictures, simply and neatly presented. Leave the fancy stuff to the traditional paste-up method, and the classically trained designers who know what they are doing; and do the simple stuff with a good word processor and a good graphics program.

Graphics Packages

Photographic manipulation can now be done to an extraordinary degree of sophistication – not in the darkroom, but on the computer screen. Once a photo is 'scanned' (turned into a series of coloured dots readable by a computer) you can do anything you like with a graphics manipulation program. Make the colours richer, the contrast better, remove the spots from the model's face; even combine two separate images perfectly to place the Prime Minister's head on a page three model's body. Thus the concept manages to appeal to both quality magazines and tabloid newspapers, for different reasons.

Typical programs: Adobe Photoshop.

Disadvantages: Because of the high density of information, graphics programs need very fast expensive machines, huge storage space, and *lots* of time to do their stuff. And the Prime Minister still does not look any better with a page three model's body.

Accounts Packages

They record your incomings and outgoings and tell you how you stand financially. This is about the most interesting thing that can be said about them.

Disadvantages: No accounts package can ever do precisely what you want. They always do VAT by default if you are doing your home accounts on it, or don't do VAT if your small business is VAT registered.

What you really need, you tell people, is a spreadsheet – then you can design your own accounts package tailored to your needs.

Spreadsheets

Spreadsheets replace the back of an envelope: you define structures (making the total at the foot of a column equal to the sum of all the figures in this column, for example), and then see what happens if you change one of the figures somewhere in the structure. Good for 'what-if?' calculations. You can usually turn your tables of figures into nice-looking pie charts, bar charts and graphs.

Typical programs: Lotus 1-2-3, things ending in '-Calc'.

Disadvantages: No-one can think what to use their spreadsheets for, or how to make them do it once they have thought of something, except produce nice-looking pie charts, bar charts and graphs. It is always best to buy a package for the specific use you have in mind; an accounts package, for example. Very good for impressing bank managers, but very little else.

Databases

They handle information – typically, name-and-address-plus-details lists for businesses or clubs. You can select certain groups, sort all the entries into order of name or amount owing you, print them out and so on. The word also means a store of information as well as the program which handles it.

Typical programs: dBase, anything ending in '-base'.

Disadvantages: You hardly ever do anything important with a database, except carry lists of names and addresses of your club members or customers. These are used to send letters to when something happens, e.g. when their subscription runs out. Instead of bothering with setting up complicated databases, it is much easier, you assert, to buy a mailmerger and deal with the letter-sending direct.

Mailmergers

These are programs which take a name and address file on the one hand and a letter with slots marked out on the other, and fill the slots appropriately with information from the address file, making a letter for each name. You can vary the contents of the letter according to information in the name and address file.

These programs send you letters beginning 'Dear Mr Johnx50n – Great news! You, Mr Johnx50n, have been selected from all the people in Lodnon to take part in our prize draw...'

Typical programs: end in '-merge', and often are included with word processors.

Disadvantages: After printing 15,000 letters to your customers you realise they read 'Dear Mr 15 High St, You have been selected from all our customers in Smith to receive...' What you really need is something which 'knows' not to put the wrong thing in the wrong place – say a database.

Games

There are so many games around that any given game will have several dozen look-alikes. So you can make up anything you like and no-one will be able to disagree with you. For example, when someone says how good this game is they have just got, you smile and say "That's just a Klarch clone isn't it? Space Sniper has more levels. Mutants of Warp Zone XXIII has better graphics. And the PC version is useless" (or "miles better", depending on their machine).

Typical programs: any game is typical.

Disadvantages: Games of old were very basic. All you had were green alien blobs who were about to invade the earth and the only way to communicate with them was to shoot them. Now, with ever more sophisticated technology, you have all colours and shapes of smoothly-animated aliens in 3-D who can play chess with you in four languages as they invade – but still all you can do is shoot them.

Graphic User Interfaces

Graphic User Interfaces (or GUIs or 'gooeys' because once you have got one you are stuck with it) are programs that allow you to run other programs (not to be confused with operating systems, which are programs that allow you to run other programs).

The first important GUI was the one that appears when you start up an Apple Mac. This was a WIMP system which meant that illiterates and dyslexics could use a computer. In an attempt to cash in on this valuable market, programmers for all kinds of computers rushed out their own versions, including, most notably, Windows for the IBM-compatible market. You can now buy programs designed to run under your GUI so software houses can, at last, offer word-processors specifically designed for people who cannot read.

Public Domain and Shareware

You can tell what cheapskates PD enthusiasts are by the fact that they do not even bother acquiring a full three-letter abbreviation. PD stands for Public Domain, a grand idea that programs should not be bought and sold in a sordid money-grabbing way, but should be given away free. Such programs are **PD,** or **freeware**.

Much is available on the Internet, and much is distributed from one user to another, free of charge.

But clubs have also been set up to distribute PD software. They give away all these programs totally free – except for the cost of membership, and a disc and, of course, a small handling charge, postage and packaging, and then there's 15 per cent service charge, and so on.

Too often the high ideals of free software are flouted in a shabby form of commercialism. In fact there is only one club that still holds to the true standards of PD, and that is the club that you are recommending.

PD clubs draw their software from a number of areas. Some people offer their programs from a real belief in the principles of PD: they have a truly useful program but do not have the money to promote it properly. Rather than sell it to a software house they unselfishly give it away in the hope of making considerably more money.

The way these people make their money is by selling you a manual. As it should be possible to run any good software without opening the manual (ask any computer journalist), the programmers go to a lot of trouble to make sure that their program cannot be run without the most obscure instructions possible. By the time they have thought up all the most unlikely key-presses, it ends up less like running a program and more like playing a Schoenberg piano sonata.

The second main source of software is the program that has been knocked up as a sure-fire commercial success but has not yet found a software company to promote it. Rather than see hours of work go down the drain it is offered to other PD enthusiasts in the hope that someone might find it useful. You may have thought some of the commercial stuff was bad, but this puts everything in perspective.

Some software is produced from similar sources to those above but on the understanding that it can be freely copied and distributed. You try it out, and if you like it you voluntarily pay some registration free to the producers. This usually involves sending $25 or so to the States. If however you do not, you erase it. **Shareware**, as it is called, clearly depends on users being honest: they could just keep it, use it, and not pay anything, especially as that $25 probably costs $25 to convert from your own currency and send. Naturally, such dishonesty never happens, just as people never make copies of commercial software from their friends or from work.

Viruses

A virus is a hidden program which gets into the system of your machine via discs you have copied something from. It copies itself on to your hard disc, and from there onto all discs you put in subsequently – and after it has reproduced a few times, does something catastrophic such as wiping your hard disc, or something mildly irritating such as announcing that it is Perry Como's birthday. By this time it is on your other discs too, and if you have lent them to anyone else, all theirs as well.

They are written by teenagers showing off, or bitter individuals looking for digital revenge on society. You can speculate about the potential disasters a bad virus might cause ("Think of the Air Traffic Control computers... hospital machines... Ministry of Defence") but for the bluffer there is nothing to fear. If you never use a computer, you cannot be affected by a virus. You can, however, worry everyone you meet. When they tell you what program they have just been using, you say "Ah, yes, they've just discovered a virus on that one. Wipes out everything you've ever done."

LANGUAGES

You can write programs in a variety of different computer languages. Professional programmers talk about 'complex' languages such as BASIC (in which the command to print a name to screen might be something very simple, PRINT NAME$, say) and 'simple' languages like assembler (in which the same command might take up 80 lines of nonsense like PUSH A and SHLD LXI,3 and LD (HL),87). The assembler version works far faster, of course – by as much as several dozen milliseconds.

BASIC, despite being frowned on by 'real' programmers, is fine for doing anything and writing in assembler is an unnecessary waste of time. Arguments for BASIC are as follows:

a) it is easy to learn,
b) it is easy to use,
c) it can do anything other languages can do, and
d) its slowness is negligible if used on a fast computer; but mainly,
e) it annoys programmers and hackers immensely to have someone refusing to run BASIC down.

Sooner or later you will have to explain to someone what the difference is between a **compiled language** and an **interpreted language** like BASIC. Put on your best I'll-put-it-in-man-in-the-street-terms voice, and say that a compiled language is like a professionally done translation and an interpreted language is like a phrase book. The latter is translated line-by-line into machine code, and like a phrase book conversation can be verbose, tautological and clumsy; the former is more efficient and elegant and will not say things twice, but clearly the phrase book version is easiest for conversation, and indeed developing a program, which involves 'talking' to your computer, is best done with an interpreted language like BASIC.

BASIC stands for Beginners All Purpose Symbolic Instruction Code, a fact you only need remember for pub quizzes. It is the language everyone starts on but those who 'move on' to other languages (the most popular is C, being easy for programmers to spell) regard it as a stage they have gone through and look down on it. If you want to program, use BASIC but don't admit to it. Everyone else does that.

Others

You need to know about generations.

First-generation languages are raw and work at a simple level on the machine, so are incredibly tedious to program with. (Machine code is first-generation: a program in machine code would read like 01001011 10010100 0001001010001001 and so on.)

Second generation is assembler.

Third generation is more sensible languages like BASIC which have almost comprehensible instructions like *PRINT TOTAL* and *STOP* and *TAX=COST*VAT RATE*, etc.

Fourth-generation languages will write a third-generation program, so you effectively say 'write me a program to total up these numbers and calculate VAT on them' and it will do it for you.

Nobody knows for sure but fifth generation programs probably sit about criticising the mistakes the fourth generation languages make in programming. This is probably something to do with artificial intelligence.

HISTORY

In computers anything 10 minutes old is out of date. Knowing the history is therefore a total waste of time. However, familiarity with a few historic milestones can impress the computer ignorant – i.e. virtually anyone.

The Babylonians invented the abacus in about 500BC, but the Greeks went further. **Eratosthenes**, for example, invented a computer program-like way of finding prime numbers in about 250BC. Realising that if they did have computers, people would then do nothing but waste their time working out endless lists of prime numbers, the Greeks wisely desisted from inventing any.

The abacus, in use in China for thousands of years, is still found in many places in the Orient today, such as Japan – usually to prop up fifth-generation computers. At this point someone usually pops up and claims that skilled abacus users can add up a column of figures faster than a calculator – four seconds for a calculator but three for an abacus. Say this is rubbish: point out that it disregards the three years spent learning how to use an abacus, making the time to add a column of figures three years and three seconds.

Calculating

Abacuses, however, are useless at multiplying (unlike the Chinese) and the mechanisation of calculation was left to Scotsman **John Napier**, who discovered logarithms around the turn of the 1600s. This proved the key to multiplication and division, and the invention of the slide rule with which to do these operations quickly and easily.

Napier is therefore a key figure to remember, partly because his contribution was important, but mainly because the words 'logarithm' and 'slide rule' (and 'Scotsman') intimidate people, stop them asking awkward questions, and make you sound confident and clever.

Blaise Pascal, son of a French tax collector, made the next step in 1642. He built a calculating machine to help his father do the tax demands. This could add and take away – mainly take away, in fact, given its purpose.

One might have thought that with a bit of imagination he could have converted the device to work with other things too, but he didn't. The reason for this omission may have been that he divided his spare time equally between lengthy sessions of self-flagellation and the activity (history does not record what activity) for which he was flagellating himself in the first place. Pascal resolved his emotional problems by entering a Jansenist convent at the age of 32, possibly as a tax dodge.

It was **Gottfried Leibnitz** thirty years later who developed the calculating machine idea into the form used right up to the 1940s, though it wasn't until the 1970s that **Clive Sinclair** brilliantly pioneered the electronic calculator (followed up with other sure fire winners such as the C5 electric car and the battery-powered Zike bike). The Leibnitz machine could multiply but only if you turned the handle the requisite number of times, making multiplication by say 255 slow, awkward and embarrassing – a bit like driving a C5.

Real Computers

However, calculation is only one facet of computing, though granted a very useful (i.e. boring) one. The real definition of a computer is something which can be programmed to do different things, such as work out prime numbers and other more interesting (i.e. completely useless and timewasting) tasks.

The breakthrough in programmed machines was a loom invented by **Joseph Jacquard** in 1805 which could weave different patterns according to which cards were fed into its controller. A pattern could be coded into a set of cards, just like a program. Unfortunately the weavers at Lyons were upset by the unemployment prospects and tried to drown him in the Rhone. You can try attributing the phrase 'collecting one's cards', meaning to be sacked, to this, though it is not true. You can also use this as a clinching argument for or against new technology in the workplace. And for or against being able to swim.

Devonshireman **Charles Babbage** is a major figure in the history of computers. Bluffers should know that he not only left his brain to the Royal College of Surgeons, but also developed two proto-computers (a good phrase to use). The '**Difference Engine**', first outlined in 1833, was steam driven and the size of a locomotive. This set many patterns for British research and development in that it was decades ahead of its time (having punched card input and printed output for example) and it was abandoned before completion through lack of money (though a model was built in Sweden). The more ambitious '**Analytical Engine**' set even more familiar standards for British design – it was never built at all.

The thing to remember is that the punch cards were prepared by the lovely Countess **Ada Lovelace**, Lord Byron's daughter, who was therefore the world's first programmer, and who set the pattern for programmers to come by taking to drink and drugs. She died young, but Babbage became quite a celebrity in his own lifetime, giving soireés for the likes of Wellington, Darwin and Carlyle, and inventing the speedometer and the cow-catcher for 'locomotives', which were steam-driven and the size of the Difference Engine.

The US census of 1890 gave rise to data processing: the idea of using machines to process vital (i.e. incredibly boring and repetitive) information. Faced with the prospect of the census results taking so long to process that they would not be ready until after the next census had been taken, the government brought in **Herman Hollerith** who put all the information on to punch cards and processed the lot in two-and-a-half years.

Hollerith realised that there was a market for processing incredibly boring information for businesses and started a company; in 1924 it became **IBM**, which now has such a high turnover that they have to keep developing new machines to keep track of their accounts.

World War II

The war is a splendid area to profess knowledge about, partly because a great many significant developments occurred, but more importantly because much information about the research is still classified, so you can say what you like and no-one can disprove it.

To break the Germans' Enigma codes, the British mathematician **Alan Turing** organised the building of the Colossus, a huge machine containing 1,500 valves. It cracked the codes, and even by today's standards it wasn't bad – it could probably decipher the conversation of a modern-day Internet user.

After the war the boffins who had been working on war computers carried on their research for more peaceful purposes. They spent most of their time thinking up acronymic names for their projects such as **ENIAC**, **EDSAC**, **ACE**, **EDVAC**, **UNIVAC**, but not **SHAKEANDVAC**.

The only important thing to remember about these is that they were all excellent for mathematical calculations, but could not do anything practical like remember a telephone number. That was not just the boffins; it was the same for the computers they designed. In those days computers, like university budgets, were much larger than today: about the size of a studio flat in London, and even more expensive.

The first 'real' computer ran its first program on 21st June 1948 at Manchester University under Alan Turing. Mention sadly that Turing was shortly after found to be a homosexual and, since this was a crime at the time, lost his funding and his job, and committed suicide. This can lead you away nicely from the subject of computers and should stop anyone asking what ENIAC, EDSAC, etc. stand for.

Business

You should know that the very first company to use real business computers was Lyons Tea who developed LEO (Lyons Electronic Office). Point out that this set two important trends: the use of computers for practical information storage and manipulation, rather than sheer academic number-crunching; but more significantly, awful puns in computing.

Technology

In 1953 there were only 100 computers in use throughout the world; now the number is many millions of times that, which you can cite as a good or bad thing. The late 1950s to the present day, you may say, is one long march of progress and developing technology.

Transistors were the first big breakthrough and meant that not only were computers smaller, but operators could listen to the radio as they worked. Punch cards were replaced by magnetic tape, meaning they could listen to their favourite pop music as well. Then huge reels of magnetic tape were replaced by small discs, which meant you could now ruin an entire disc by spilling a single cup of coffee, whereas before you could only ruin a couple of inches of tape. The advent of microprocessors, in which many thousands of transistors could be put on to a chip of silicon, spawned the growth of the microcomputer industry in the late 70s and early 80s, and meant that a spilt coffee could now ruin an entire computer.

The pioneers of the microcomputer revolution were Commodore, who made the coyly named PET; Tandy, known in America as Radio Shack, who made the TRS 80; and Apple, who made the Apple.

Apple I was put together in a garage by **Steve Jobs** and **Steve Wozniak** – who had earlier made a living by selling devices that helped phone-freaks (phreaks) to tap into the USA national telephone network. It cost a few hundred dollars to develop and was named Apple because no-one could think of a better name by five o'clock on the day when the company had to post off its official registration form; with amazing foresight, the name proved ideal for yet more appalling puns ('another byte of the Apple', 'Apples don't grow on trees', 'Apple pipped', etc.).

In 1977 sales of Apple II were $2.5 million; in 1982 sales were $583 million. Jobs and Wozniak became multi-millionaires long before reaching thirty.

However, this is small change compared to the multiple billions of **Bill Gates**, the Harvard drop out who heads Microsoft and is the man behind PC standards such as Word and Windows.

Gates knows everything about computers, whereas Britain's most successful computer pioneer of recent years, **Alan Sugar** of Amstrad fame, confesses to understanding practically nothing about them. Suggest that the cultivation of this complete lack of computing expertise is an advantage in that an interest in technical matters is never allowed to cloud an individual's commercial judgment.

GLOSSARY

Address – Where a byte lives in memory lane. Expressed as combinations like C84A or B20E; this is the PC, supposedly 'program counter' but clearly really the postcode.

Bug – For example, when you press the f3 key and find it doesn't reformat your document as promised, but unexpectedly erases your hard disc. A bug is something that doesn't work as it should – like the software testers employed to spot them.

Byte – Just enough space inside a computer to store one letter, or number below 255, i.e. just one bit of information – except that a byte is 8 bits.

CAD – 'Computer Aided Design', the idea of doing your technical drawing on computer instead of on paper. Also stands for 'Crude And Disappointing'.

CD–ROM – Software in CD form, with vast storage capacity; on an audio CD player it only produces meaningless whines and squeaks, so must not be confused with your Stockhausen discs.

Crash – To stop working irretrievably, the only remedy being to switch off and start again. Opposite of the Stock Market crash, which was caused by hyperactive computers endlessly selling to each other.

Data – Just means 'facts and figures', but arguably either singular or plural in English, so whatever version the other person uses, say they're wrong.

Endless loop – See 'Infinite loop'.

File – Any single thing stored on a disc: a program, some data for a program (say details about your stock of nails, which would be nail file) or a text document like a recipe (in which case you can put a cake in a file).

Hardware – Computer equipment, as opposed to software (programs). The difference is that you can't steal hardware by slipping it into your pocket.

Icon – Representation of something onscreen by a picture, instead of words, because of games players' dubious literacy.

Infinite loop – See 'Endless loop'.

Internet – More realistic name for **information superhighway**. Like real highways, parts get closed off unexpectedly and popular routes are always jammed solid.

K – 'Kilobyte'. Measurement of space on a disc (a letter to your bank would take up 1-2k, this book 100-110k). Equal to 1024 characters, from Greek 'kilo' meaning '1000', because nobody knew what '1024' was in Greek.

Mb – Short for 'megabyte'. One thousand k. Or is it 1024k, i.e. 1024000 characters? Or maybe 1024 x 1024 = 1048576, or perhaps just 1000000. Not even *War and Peace* is as big as a megabyte.

Menu – List of options given in your program just like a restaurant menu, i.e. everything has misleading names and what you want is never available.

Modem – Device enabling your computer to link up to the phone network at great expense and do things from your screen, like pay phone bills.

Mouse – Hand-size device which runs on a ball and moves a pointer on the screen; by clicking the mouse button you can activate the thing pointed to. Make people believe it's an acronym for 'Manually Operated Utility Selection Equipment'. It isn't. Computer people really thought that 'mice' looked like mice.

Recursion – See 'Recursion'.

RAM – Wherever you are, you should remember that this is Random Access Memory.

REM – Instruction put at the beginning of a line in a program to make the computer ignore that line. However even beginners can usually put something into a line that can cause the computer to ignore all the lines in the program.

ROM – Read Only Memory, such as that on CD-based software: two ROMs do not make a write.

RUM – Popular device with programmers: a drink made from fermented sugar-cane juice.

Upgrade – Improved version of a program with the old bugs taken out and new ones put in.

World Wide Web – The graphical system that enables users to fly around the Internet – and, like real flies in a web, get caught and pay dearly for it.

THE AUTHORS

The co-authors of this book met while working for the same monthly computer magazine, *8000 Plus* – once at the cutting edge, but now rather outdated and superseded by younger rivals, facing an uncertain future. The authors, that is. The magazine is still going strong.

Alexander Rae is a world-weary Glaswegian ex-journalist, with a wife and two violent children. His age is 29, but only in hex. After years as a public relations executive for a multi-national industrial conglomerate, he now bluffs professionally in his own computer training, public relations and freelance writing business – he has a very short concentration span.

Rob Ainsley edited computer magazines before leaving for *Classic CD*, a classical music monthly. However, much of his writing is still directed towards computer magazines – mostly letters demanding payment for articles published two years ago. His computer at work is on e-mail and can therefore be accessed by computer buffs from all over the world, which is why he spends so much time working at home. Nearly 30, but not from the right direction, he lives in Bath.

This book was produced on an Apple Macintosh and sent direct by modem to the publishers½3 ad is a4 exmple 11nw tech – 4e½!mzThis book was wr

THE BLUFFER'S GUIDES®

Available at £1.99* and £2.50 each:

Accountancy
Advertising
Antiques*
Archaeology
Astrology & Fortune Telling*
Ballet*
Bluffing
British Class*
Champagne
Chess
The Classics
Computers
Consultancy
Cricket
Doctoring
Economics
The European Union
Finance
The Flight Deck
Golf
The Internet
Jazz
Journalism*
Law
Literature*
Management
Marketing

Maths*
Modern Art
Music
The Occult*
Opera
Paris
Philosophy
Photography*
Poetry*
P.R.
Public Speaking
Publishing*
The Quantum Universe
The Races
The Rock Music Business
Rugby
Science
Secretaries
Seduction
Sex
Skiing
Small Business
Teaching
Theatre*
University
Whisky
Wine

All these books are available at your local bookshop or newsagent, or by post or telephone from: B.B.C.S., P.O.Box 941, Hull HU1 3VQ. (24 hour Telephone Credit Card Line: 01482 224626)

Please add the following for postage charges: UK (& BFPO) Orders: £1.00 for the first book & 50p for each additional book up to a maximum of £2.50; Overseas (& Eire) Orders: £2.00 for the first book, £1.00 for the second & 50p for each additional book.